On Two Souls,
Against the Manichaeans

On Two Souls, Against the Manichaeans

St. Augustine

On Two Souls, Against the Manichaeans

© Lighthouse Publishing 2018

Written by: St. Augustine (Nov.13 354 – Aug.28 430)

Translated by: Albert H. Newman, D.D., L.L.D

Updated into Modern U.S English by A.M. Overett (b. 1960)

All rights reserved. Without limiting the rights under copyright reserved above, no part of this publication may be reproduced, stored in a retrieval system, or transmitted, in any form or by any means (electronic, mechanical, photocopying, recording or otherwise), without the prior written permission of the copyright owner of this book.

Published by
Lighthouse Christian Publishing
SAN 257-4330
5531 Dufferin Drive
Savage, Minnesota, 55378
United States of America

www.lighthousechristianpublishing.com

Chapter 1. —By What Course of Reasoning the Error of the Manichæans Concerning Two Souls, One of Which is Not from God, is Refuted. Every Soul, Inasmuch as It is a Certain Life, Can Have Its Existence Only from God the Source of Life.

1. Through the assisting mercy of God, the snares of the Manichæans having been broken to pieces and left behind, having been restored at length to the bosom of the Catholic Church, I am disposed now at least to consider and to deplore my recent wretchedness. For there were many things that I ought to have done to prevent the seeds of the most true religion wholesomely implanted in me from boyhood, from being banished from my mind, having been uprooted by the error and fraud of false and deceitful men. For, in the first place, if I had soberly and diligently considered, with prayerful and pious mind, those two kinds of souls to which they attributed natures and properties so distinct that they wished one to be regarded as of the very substance of God, but were not even willing that God should be accepted as the author of the other; perhaps it would have appeared to me, intent on learning, that there is no life whatsoever, which, by the very fact of its being life and in so far as it is life at all, does not pertain to the supreme source and beginning of life, which we must acknowledge to be nothing else than the supreme and only and true God. Wherefore there is no reason why we should not confess, that those souls which the Manichæans call evil are either devoid of life and so not souls, neither will anything positively or negatively, neither follow after nor flee from anything; or, if they live so that they can be souls, and act as the Manichæans suppose, in no way do they live unless by

life, and if it be an established fact, as it is, that Christ has said: "I am the life," that all souls seeing that they cannot be souls except by living were created and fashioned by Christ, that is, by the Life.

Chapter 2. —If the Light that is Perceived by Sense Has God for Its Author, as the Manichæans Acknowledge, Much More The Soul Which is Perceived by Intellect Alone.

2. But if at that time my thought was not able to bear and sustain the question concerning life and partaking of life, which is truly a great question, and one that requires much calm discussion among the learned, I might perchance have had power to discover that which to every man considering himself, without a study of the individual parts, is perfectly evident, namely, that everything we are said to know and to understand, we comprehend either by bodily sense or by mental operation. That the five bodily senses are commonly enumerated as sight, hearing, smell, taste, touch, than all of which intellect is immeasurably more noble and excellent, who would have been so ungrateful and impious as not to concede to me; which being established and confirmed, we should have seen how it follows, that whatsoever things are perceived by touch or sight or in any bodily manner at all, are by so much inferior to those things that we comprehend intellectually as the senses are inferior to the intellect. Wherefore, since all life, and so every soul, can be perceived by no bodily sense, but by the intellect alone, whereas while yonder sun and moon and every luminary that is beheld by these mortal eyes, the Manichæans themselves also say must be attributed to

the true and good God, it is the height of madness to claim that that belongs to God which we observe bodily; but, on the other hand, to think that what we receive not only by the mind, but by the highest form of mind, namely, reason and intellect, that is life, whatsoever it may be called, nevertheless life, should be deprived and bereft of the same God as its author. For if having invoked God, I had asked myself what living is, how inscrutable it is to every bodily sense, how absolutely incorporeal it is, could not I have answered? Or would not the Manichæans also confess not only that the souls they detest live, but that they live also immortally? and that Christ's saying: "Send the dead to bury their dead," was uttered not with reference to those not living at all, but with reference to sinners, which is the only death of the immortal soul; as when Paul writes: "The widow that gives herself to pleasure is dead while she lives," he says that she at the same time is dead, and alive. Wherefore I should have directed attention not to the great degree of contamination in which the sinful soul lives, but only to the fact itself that it lives. But if I cannot perceive except by an act of intelligence, I believe it would have come into the mind, that by as much as any mind whatever is to be preferred to the light which we see through these eyes, by so much we should give to intellect the preference over the eyes themselves.

Chapter 3. —How It is Proved that Every Body Also is from God. That the Soul Which is Called Evil by the Manichæans is Better Than Light.

They also affirm that the light is from the Father of Christ: should I then have doubted that every soul is from Him? But not even then, as a man forsooth so inexperienced and so youthful as I was, should I have been in doubt as to the derivation not only of the soul, but also of the body, nay of everything whatsoever, from Him, if I had reverently and cautiously reflected on what form is, or what has been formed, what shape is and what has been endued with shape.

3. But not to speak at present concerning the body, I lament concerning the soul, concerning spontaneous and vivid movement, concerning action, concerning life, concerning immortality; in fine, I lament that I, miserable, should have believed that anything could have all these properties apart from the goodness of God, which properties, great as they are, I sadly neglected to consider; this I think, should be to me a matter of groaning and of weeping. I should have inwardly pondered these things, I should have discussed them with myself, I should have referred them to others, I should have propounded the inquiry, what the power of knowing is, seeing there is nothing in man that we can compare to this excellency? And as men, if only they had been men, would have granted me this, I should have inquired whether seeing with these eyes is knowing? In case they had answered negatively, I should first have concluded, that mental intelligence is vastly inferior to ocular sensation; then I should have added, that what we perceive by means of a better thing must needs be judged to be itself better. Who would not grant this? I should have gone on to inquire, whether that soul which they call evil is an object of ocular sensation or of mental intelligence? They would have acknowledged that the latter is the case. All which things having been agreed upon and confirmed between us, I should have shown

how it follows, that that soul forsooth which they execrate, is better than that light which they venerate, since the former is an object of mental knowledge, the latter an object of corporeal sense perception. But here perhaps they would have halted, and would have refused to follow the lead of reason, so great is the power of inveterate opinion and of falsehood long defended and believed. But I should have pressed yet more upon them halting, not harshly, not in puerile fashion, not obstinately; I should have repeated the things that had been conceded, and have shown how they must be conceded. I should have exhorted that they consult in common, that they may see clearly what must be denied to us; whether they think it false that intellectual perception is to be preferred to these carnal organs of sight, or that what is known by means of the excellency of the mind is more excellent than what is known by vile corporeal sensation; whether they would be unwilling to confess that those souls which they think heterogenous, can be known only by intellectual perception, that is, by the excellency itself of the mind; whether they would wish to deny that the sun and the moon are made known to us only by means of these eyes. But if they had replied that no one of these things could be denied otherwise than most absurdly and most impudently, I should have urged that they ought not to doubt but that the light whose worthiness of worship they proclaim, is viler than that soul which they admonish men to flee.

Chapter 4. —Even the Soul of a Fly is More Excellent Than the Light.

4. And here, if perchance in their confusion they

had inquired of me whether I thought that the soul even of a fly surpasses that light, I should have replied, yes, nor should it have troubled me that the fly is little, but it should have confirmed me that it is alive. For it is inquired, what causes those members so diminutive to grow, what leads so minute a body here and there according to its natural appetite, what moves its feet in numerical order when it is running, what regulates and gives vibration to its wings when flying? This thing whatever it is in so small a creature towers up so prominently to one well considering, that it excels any lightning flashing upon the eyes.

Chapter 5. —How Vicious Souls, However Worthy of Condemnation They May Be, Excel the Light Which is Praiseworthy in Its Kind.

Certainly, nobody doubts that whatever is an object of intellectual perception, by virtue of divine laws surpasses in excellence every sensible object and consequently also this light. For what, I ask, do we perceive by thought, if not that it is one thing to know with the mind, and another thing to experience bodily sensations, and that the former is incomparably more sublime than the latter, and so that intelligible things must needs be preferred to sensible things, since the intellect itself is so highly exalted above the senses?

5. Hence this also I should perchance have known, which manifestly follows, since injustice and intemperance and other vices of the mind are not objects of sense, but of intellect, how it comes about that these too which we detest and consider condemnable, yet in as much as they are objects of intellect, can outrank this light

however praiseworthy it may be in its kind. For it is borne in upon the mind subjecting itself well to God, that, first of all, not everything that we praise is to be preferred to everything that we find fault with. For in praising the purest lead, I do not therefore put a higher value upon it than upon the gold that I find fault with. For everything must be considered in its kind. I disapprove of a lawyer ignorant of many statutes, yet I so prefer him to the most approved tailor, that I should think him incomparably superior. But I praise the tailor because he is thoroughly skilled in his own craft, while I rightly blame the lawyer because he imperfectly fulfills the functions of his profession. Wherefore I should have found out that the light which in its own kind is perfect, is rightly to be praised; yet because it is included in the number of sensible things, which class must needs yield to the class of intelligible things, it must be ranked below unjust and intemperate souls, since these are intelligible; although we may without injustice judge these to be most worthy of condemnation. For in the case of these we ask that they be reconciled to God, not that they be preferred to that lightning. Wherefore, if anyone had contended that this luminary is from God, I should not have opposed; but rather I should have said, that souls, even vicious ones, not in so far as they are vicious, but in so far as they are souls, must be acknowledged to be creatures of God.

Chapter 6. —Whether Even Vices Themselves as Objects of Intellectual Apprehension are to Be Preferred to Light as an Object of Sense Perception, and are to Be Attributed to God as Their Author. Vice of the Mind and Certain Defects are Not Rightly to Be Counted Among Intelligible Things. Defects Themselves Even If They Should Be Counted Among Intelligible Things Should Never Be Put Before Sensible Things. If Light is Visible by God, Much More is the Soul, Even If Vicious, Which in So Far as It Lives is an Intelligible Thing. Passages of Scripture are Adduced by the Manichæans to the Contrary.

At this point, in case someone of them, cautious and watchful, now also more studious than pertinacious, had admonished me that the inquiry is not about vicious souls but about vices themselves, which, seeing that they are not known by corporeal sense, and yet are known, can only be received as objects of intellectual apprehension, which if they excel all objects of sense, why can we not agree in attributing light to God as its author, but only a sacrilegious person would say that God is the author of vices; I should have replied to the man, if either on the spur of the moment, as is customary to the worshippers of the good God, a solution of this question had darted like lightning from on high, or a solution had been previously prepared. If I had not deserved or was unable to avail myself of either of these methods, I should have deferred the undertaking, and should have confessed that the thing propounded was difficult to discern and arduous. I should have withdrawn to myself, prostrated myself before God, groaned aloud asking Him not to suffer me to halt in mid space, when I should have moved forward with assured arguments, asking Him that I might not be compelled by a doubtful question either to subordinate intelligible things to sensible, and to yield, or to call Himself the author of vices; since either of these alternatives would have been absolutely full of falsehood and impiety. I can by no means suppose that He would have deserted me in such a frame of mind. Rather, in His own ineffable way, He would have admonished me to consider again and again whether vices of mind concerning which I was so troubled should be reckoned among intelligible things. But that I might find out, because the weakness of my inner eye, which rightly befell me on account of my sins, I should have devised some sort of stage for gazing upon spiritual things in visible things themselves, of which we have by no means a surer knowledge, but a more confident familiarity. Therefore I should straightway have inquired, what properly pertains to the sensation of the eyes. I should have found that it is the color, the dominion of which the light holds. For these are the things that no other sense touches, for the motions and magnitudes and intervals and figures of bodies, although they also can be perceived by the eyes, yet to perceive such is not their peculiar function, but belongs also to touch. Whence I should have gathered that by as much as yonder light excels other corporeal and sensible things, by so much is sight more noble than the other senses. The light therefore having been selected from all the things that are perceived by bodily sense, by this [light] I should have striven, and in this of necessity I should have placed that stage of my inquiry. I should have gone on to consider what might be done in this way, and thus I should have reasoned with myself: If yonder sun, conspicuous by its brightness and sufficing for day by its light, should little by little decline in our sight into the likeness of the moon, would we perceive anything else with our eyes than light however refulgent, yet seeking light by reason of not seeing what had been, and using it for seeing what was present? Therefore we should not see the decline, but the light that should survive the decline. But since we should not see, we should not perceive; for whatever we perceive by sight must necessarily be seen; wherefore if that decline were perceived neither by sight nor by any other sense, it cannot be reckoned among objects of sense. For nothing is an object of sense that cannot be perceived by sense. Let us apply now the consideration to virtue, by whose intellectual light we most fittingly say the mind shines. Again, a certain decline from this light of virtue, not destroying the soul, but obscuring it, is called vice. Therefore also vice can by no means be reckoned among objects of intellectual perception, as that decline of light is rightly excluded from the number of objects of sense perception. Yet what remains of soul, that is that which lives and is soul is just as much an object of intellectual perception as that is an object of sense perception which should shine in this visible luminary after any imaginable degree of decline. And so the soul, in so far as it is soul and partakes of life, without which it can in no way be soul, is most correctly to be preferred to all objects of sense perception. Wherefore it is most erroneous to say that any soul is not from God, from whom you boast that the sun and moon have their existence.

7. But if now it should be thought fit to designate as objects of sense perception not only all those things that we perceive by the senses, but also all those things that though not perceiving by the senses we judge of by

means of the body, as of darkness through the eyes, of silence through the ears,—for not by seeing darkness and not by hearing silence do we know of their existence,— and again, in the case of objects of intellectual perception, not those things only which we see illuminated by the mind, as is wisdom itself, but also those things which by the illumination itself we avoid, such as foolishness, which I might fittingly designate mental darkness; I should have made no controversy about a word, but should have dissolved the whole question by an easy division, and straightway I should have proved to those giving good attention, that by the divine law of truth intelligible subsistence are to be preferred to sensible subsistence, not the decline of these subsistence, even though we should choose to call these intelligible, those sensible. Wherefore, that those who acknowledge that these visible luminaries and those intelligible souls are subsistence, are in every way compelled to grant and to attribute the sublimer part to souls; but that defects of either kind cannot be preferred the one to the other, for they are only privative and indicate nonexistence, and therefore have precisely the same force as negations themselves. For when we say, It is not gold, and, It is not virtue, although there is the greatest possible difference between gold and virtue, yet there is no difference between the negations that we adjoin to them. But that it is worse indeed not to be virtue than not to be gold, no sane man doubts. Who does not know that the difference lies not in the negations themselves, but in the things to which they are adjoined? For by as much as virtue is more excellent than gold, by so much is it more wretched to be in want of virtue than of gold. Wherefore, since intelligible things excel sensible things, we rightly feel greater repugnance towards defect in intelligible than in sensible things, esteeming not the defects, but the things that are deficient more or less precious. From which now it appears, that defect of light, which is intelligible, is far more wretched than defect of the sensible light, because, forsooth, life which is known is by far more precious than yonder light which is seen.

8. This being the case, who will dare, while attributing sun and moon, and whatever is refulgent in the stars, nay in this fire of ours and in this visible earthly life, to God, to decline to grant that any souls whatsoever, which are not souls except by the fact of their being perfectly alive, since in this fact alone life has the precedence of light, are from God. And since he speaks truth who says, In as far as a thing shines it is from God, would I speak falsely, mighty God, if I should say, In so far as a thing lives it is from God? Let not, I beseech thee, blindness of intellect and perversions of mind be increased to such an extent that men may fail to know these things. But however great their error and pertinacity might have been, trusting in these arguments and armed therewith, I believe that when I should have laid the matter before them thus considered and canvassed, and should have calmly conferred with them, I should have feared lest anyone of them should have seemed to me to be of any consequence, should he endeavor to subordinate or even to compare to bodily sense, or to those things that pertain to bodily sense as objects of knowledge, either intellect or those things that are perceived (not by way of defect) by the intellect. Which point having been settled, how would he or any other have dared to deny that such souls as he would consider evil, yet since they are souls, are to be reckoned in the number of intelligible things, nor

are objects of intellectual perception by way of defect? This is on the supposition that souls are souls only by being alive. For if they were intellectually perceived as vicious through defect, being vicious by lack of virtue, yet they are perceived as souls not through defect, for they are souls because of being alive. Nor can it be maintained that presence of life is a cause of defect, for by as much as anything is defective, by so much is it severed from life.

9. Since therefore it would have been every way evident that no souls can be separated from that Author from whom yonder light is not separated, whatever they might have now adduced I should not have accepted, and should rather have admonished them that they should choose with me to follow those who maintain that whatever is, since it is, and in whatever degree it is, has its existence from the one God.

Chapter 7. —How Evil Men are of God, and Not of God.

They might have cited against me those words of the gospel: "Ye therefore do not hear, because ye are not of God;" "Ye are of your father the devil." I also should have cited: "All things were made by Him and without Him was not anything made," and this of the Apostle: "One God of whom are all things, and one Lord Jesus Christ through whom are all things," and again from the same Apostle: "Of whom are all things, through whom are all things, in whom are all things, to Him be glory." I should have exhorted those men (if indeed I had found them men), that we should presume upon nothing as if we had found it out, but should rather inquire of the masters who would demonstrate the agreement and harmony of those passages that seem to be discordant. For when in one and the same Scriptural authority we read: "All things are of God," and elsewhere: "Ye are not of God," since it is wrong rashly to condemn books of Scripture, who would not have seen that a skilled teacher should be found who would know a solution of this problem, from whom assuredly if endowed with good intellectual powers, and a "spiritual man," as is said by divine inspiration (for he would necessarily have favored the true arguments concerning the intelligible and sensible nature, which, as far as I can, I have conducted and handled, nay he would have disclosed them far better and more convincingly); we should have heard nothing else concerning this problem, except, as might happen, that there is no class of souls but has its existence from God, and that it is yet rightly said to sinners and unbelievers: "Ye are not of God." For we also, perchance, Divine aid having been implored, should have been able easily to see, that it is one thing to live and another to sin, and (although life in sin may be called death in comparison with just life, and while in one man it may be found, that he is at the same time alive and a sinner) that so far as he is alive, he is of God, so far as he is a sinner he is not of God. In which division we use that alternative that suits our sentiment; so that when we wish to insist upon the omnipotence of God as Creator, we may say even to sinners that they are of God. For we are speaking to those who are contained in some class, we are speaking to those having animal life, we are speaking to rational beings, we are speaking lastly—and this applies especially to the matter in hand—to living beings, all which things are essentially divine functions. But when our purpose is to convict evil men, we rightly say: "Ye are not of God."

For we speak to them as averse to truth, unbelieving, criminal, infamous, and, to sum up all in one term—sinners, all of which things are undoubtedly not of God. Therefore what wonder is it, if Christ says to sinners, convicting them of this very thing that they were sinners and did not believe in Him: "Ye are not of God;" and on the other hand, without prejudice to the former statement: "All things were made through Him," and "All things are of God?" For if not to believe Christ, to repudiate Christ's advent, not to accept Christ, was a sure mark of souls that are not of God; and so it was said: "Ye therefore hear not, because ye are not of God;" how would that saying of the apostle be true that occurs in the memorable beginning of the gospel: "He came unto his own things, and his own people did not receive him?" Whence his own if they did not receive him; or whence therefore not his own because they did not receive him, unless that sinners by virtue of being men belong to God, but by virtue of being sinners belong to the devil? He who says: "His own people received him not" had reference to nature; but he who says: "Ye are not of God." had reference to will; for the evangelist was commending the works of God, Christ was censuring the sins of men.

Chapter 8. —The Manichæans Inquire Whence is

Evil and by This Question Think They Have Triumphed. Let Them First Know, Which is Most Easy to Do, that Nothing Can Live Without God. Consummate Evil Cannot Be Known Except by the Knowledge of Consummate Good, Which is God.

Here perchance someone may say: Whence are sins themselves, and whence is evil in general? If from man, whence is man? if from an angel, whence is the angel? When it is said, however truly and rightly, that these are from God, it nevertheless seems to those unskillful and possessed of little power to consider recondite matters, that evils and sins are thereby connected, as by a sort of chain, to God. By this question they think themselves triumphant, as if forsooth to ask were to know; —would it were so, for in that case no one would be more knowing than myself. Yet very often in controversy the propounder of a great question, while impersonating the great teacher, is himself more ignorant in the matter concerning which he would frighten his opponent, than he whom he would frighten. These therefore suppose that they are superior to the common run, because the former ask questions that the latter cannot answer. If therefore when I most unfortunately was associated with them, not in the position in which I have now for some time been, they had raised these objections when I had brought forward this argument, I should have said: I ask that you meanwhile agree with me, which is most easy, that if nothing can shine without God, much less can anything live without God. Let us not persist in such monstrous opinions as to maintain that any souls whatsoever have life apart from God. For perchance it may so happen that with me you are ignorant as to this thing, namely whence is evil, let us then learn either simultaneously or in any order, I care not what. For what if knowledge of the perfection of evil is impossible to man without knowledge of the perfection of good? For we should not know darkness if we were always in darkness. But the notion of light does not allow its opposite to be unknown. But the highest good is that than which there is nothing higher. But God is good and than Him nothing can be higher. God therefore is the highest good. Let us therefore together so recognize God, and thus what we seek too hastily will not be hidden from us. Do you suppose then that the knowledge of God is a matter of small account or desert? For what other reward is there for us than life eternal, which is to know God? For God the Master says: "But this is life eternal, that they might know Thee the only and true God, and Jesus Christ whom thou hast sent." For the soul, although it is immortal, yet because aversion from the knowledge of God is rightly called its death, when it is converted to God, the reward of eternal life to be attained is that knowledge; so that this is, as has been said, eternal life. But no one can be converted to God, except he turn himself away from this world. This for myself I feel to be arduous and exceedingly difficult, whether it is easy to you, God Himself would have seen. I should have been inclined to think it easy to you, had I not been moved by the fact, that, since the world from which we are commanded to turn away is visible, and the apostle says: "The things that are seen are temporal, but the things that are unseen are eternal," you ascribe more importance to the judgment of these eyes than to that of the mind, asserting and believing as you do that there is no shining feather that does not shine from God; and that there are living souls that do not live from God. These and like things I should either have said to them or considered with myself, for even then, supplicating God with all my bowels, so to speak, and examining as attentively as possible the Scriptures, I should perchance have been able either to say such things or to think them, so far as was necessary for my salvation.

Chapter 9. —Augustin Deceived by Familiarity with the Manichæans, and by the Succession of Victories Over Ignorant Christians Reported by Them. The Manichæans are Likewise Easily Refuted from the Knowledge of Sin and the Will.

But two things especially, which easily lay hold upon that unwary age, urged me through wonderful circuits. One of these was familiarity, suddenly, by a certain false semblance of goodness, wrapped many times around my neck as a certain sinuous chain. The other was, that I was almost always noxiously victorious in arguing with ignorant Christians who yet eagerly attempted, each as he could, to defend their faith. By which frequent success the ardor of youth was kindled, and by its own impulse rashly verged upon the great evil of stubbornness. For this kind of wrangling, after I had become an auditor among them, whatever I was able to do either by my own genius, such as it was, or by reading the works of others, I most gladly devoted to them alone. Accordingly from their speeches ardor in disputations was daily increased, from success in disputations love for them [the Manichæans]. Whence it resulted that whatever they said, as if affected by certain strange disorders, I approved of as true, not because I knew it to be true, but because I wished it to be. So it came about that, however slowly and cautiously, yet for a long time I followed men that preferred a sleek straw to a living soul.

12. So be it, I was not able at that time to distinguish and discern sensible from intelligible things, carnal forsooth from spiritual. It did not belong to age, nor to discipline, nor even to any habit, nor, finally, to any deserts; for it is a matter of no small joy and felicitation: had I not thus been able at length even to grasp that which in the judgment of all men nature itself by the laws of the most High God has established?

Chapter 10. —Sin is Only from the Will. His Own Life and Will Best Known to Each Individual. What Will is.

For let any men whatever, if only no madness has broken them loose from the common sense of the human race, bring whatever zeal they like for judging, whatever ignorance, nay whatever slowness of mind, I should like to find out what they would have replied to me had I asked, whether a man would seem to them to have sinned by whose hand while he was asleep another should have written something disgraceful? Who doubts that they would have denied that it is a sin, and have exclaimed against it so vehemently that they might perchance have been enraged that I should have thought them proper objects of such a question? Of whom reconciled and restored to equanimity, as best I could do it, I should have begged that they would not take it amiss if I asked them another thing just as manifest, just as completely within the knowledge of all. Then I should have asked, if some stronger person had done some evil thing by the hand of one not sleeping but conscious, yet with the rest of his members bound and in constraint, whether because he knew it, though absolutely unwilling, he should be held guilty of any sin? And here all marveling that I should ask such questions, would reply without hesitation, that he had absolutely not sinned at all. Why so? Because whoever has done anything evil by means of one unconscious or unable to resist, the latter can by no means be justly condemned. And precisely why this is so, if I should inquire of the human nature in these men, I should easily bring out the desired answer, by asking in this manner: Suppose that the sleeper already knew what the other would do with his hand, and of purpose aforethought, having drunk so much as would prevent his being awakened, should go to sleep, in order to deceive someone with an oath. Would any amount of sleep suffice to prove his innocence? What else than a guilty man would one pronounce him? But if he has also willingly been bound that he may deceive someone by this pretext, in what respect then would those chains profit as a means of relieving him of sin? Although bound by these he was really not able to resist, as in the other case the sleeper was absolutely ignorant of what he was then doing. Is there therefore any possibility of doubting that both should be judged to have sinned? Which things having been conceded, I should have argued, that sin is indeed nowhere but in the will, since this consideration also would have helped me, that justice holds guilty those sinning by evil will alone, although they may have been unable to accomplish what they willed.

13. For who could have said that, in adducing these considerations, I was dwelling upon obscure and recondite things, where because the fewness of those able

to understand, either fraud or suspicion of ostentation is accustomed to arise? Let that distinction between intelligible and sensible things withdraw for a little: let me not be found fault with for following up slow minds with the stimuli of subtle disputations. Permit me to know that I live, permit me to know that I will to live. If in this the human race agrees, as our life is known to us, so also is our will. Nor when we become possessed of this knowledge, is there any occasion to fear lest anyone should convince us that we may be deceived; for no one can be deceived as to whether he does not live, or wishes nothing. I do not think that I have adduced anything obscure, and my concern is rather lest some should find fault with me for dwelling on things that are too manifest. But let us consider the bearing of these things.

14. Sinning therefore takes place only by exercise of will. But our will is very well known to us; for neither should I know that I will, if I did not know what will itself is. Accordingly, it is thus defined: will is a movement of mind, no one compelling, either for not losing or for obtaining something. Why therefore could not I have so defined it then? Was it difficult to see that one unwilling is contrary to one willing, just as the left hand is contrary to the right, not as black to white? For the same thing cannot be at the same time black and white. But whoever is placed between two men is on the left hand with reference to one, on the right with reference to the other. One man is both on the right hand and on the left hand at the same time, but by no means both to the one man. So indeed, one mind may be at the same time unwilling and willing, but it cannot be at the same time unwilling and willing with reference to one and the same thing. For when any one unwillingly does anything; if you ask him

whether he wished to do it, he says that he did not. Likewise, if you ask whether he wished not to do it, he replies that he did. So you will find him unwilling with reference to doing, willing with reference to not doing, that is to say, one mind at the same time having both attitudes, but each referring to different things. Why do I say this? Because if we should again ask wherefore though unwilling he does this, he will say that he is compelled. For everyone also who does a thing unwillingly is compelled, and everyone who is compelled, if he does a thing, does it only unwillingly. It follows that he that is willing is free from compulsion, even if anyone thinks himself compelled. And in this manner everyone who willingly does a thing is not compelled, and whoever is not compelled, either does it willingly or not at all. Since nature itself proclaims these things in all men whom we can interrogate without absurdity, from the boy even to the old man, from literary sport even to the throne of the wise, why then should I not have seen that in the definition of will should be put, "no one compelling," which now as if with greater experience most cautiously I have done. But if this is everywhere manifest, and promptly occurs to all not by instruction but by nature, what is there left that seems obscure, unless perchance it be concealed from someone, that when we wish for something, we will, and our mind is moved towards it, and we either have it or do not have it, and if we have it we will to retain it, if we have it not, to acquire it? Wherefore everyone who wills, wills either not to lose something or to obtain it. Hence if all these things are clearer than day, as they are, nor are they given to my conception alone, but by the liberality of truth itself to the whole human race, why could I not have said even at that time: Will is a movement of the mind, no one compelling, either for not losing or for obtaining something?

Chapter 11. —What Sin is.

Someone will say: What assistance would this have furnished you against the Manichæans? Wait a moment; permit me first also to define sin, which, every mind reads divinely written in itself, cannot exist apart from will. Sin therefore is the will to retain and follow after what justice forbids, and from which it is free to abstain. Although if it be not free, it is not will. But I have preferred to define more roughly than precisely. Should I not also have carefully examined those obscure books, whence I might have learned that no one is worthy of blame or punishment who either wills what justice does not prohibit him from willing, or does not do what he is not able to do? Do not shepherds on mountains, poets in theatres, unlearned in social intercourse, learned in libraries, masters in schools, priests in consecrated places, and the human race throughout the whole world, sing out these things? But if no one is worthy of blame and condemnation, who either does not act against the prohibition of justice, or who does not do what he cannot do, yet every sin is blameworthy and condemnable, who doubts then that it is sin, when willing is unjust, and not willing is free. And hence that definition is both true and easy to understand, and not only now but then also could have been spoken by me: Sin is the will of retaining or of obtaining, what justice forbids, and whence it is free to abstain?

Chapter 12. —From the Definitions Given of Sin and Will, He Overthrows the Entire Heresy of the Manichæans. Likewise from the Just Condemnation of Evil Souls It Follows that They are Evil Not by Nature But by Will. That Souls are Good By Nature, to Which the Pardon of Sins is Granted.

16. Come now, let us see in what respect these things would have aided us. Much every way, so that I should have desired nothing more; for they end the whole cause; for whoever consulting in the inner mind, where they are more pronounced and assured, the secrets of his own conscience, and the divine laws absolutely imposed upon nature, grants that these two definitions of will and sin are true, condemns without any hesitation by the fewest and the briefest, but plainly the most invincible reasons, the whole heresy of the Manichæans. Which can be thus considered. They say that there are two kinds of souls, the one good, which is in such a way from God, that it is said not to have been made by Him out of any material or out of nothing, but to have proceeded as a certain part from the very substance itself of God; the other evil, which they believe and strive to get others to believe pertains to God in no way whatever; and so they maintain that the one is the perfection of good, but the other the perfection of evil, and that these two classes were at one time distinct but are now commingled. The character and the cause of this commingling I had not yet heard; but nevertheless I could have inquired whether that evil kind of souls, before it was mingled with the good, had any will. For if not, it was without sin and innocent, and so by no means evil. But if evil in such a way, that though without will, as fire, yet if it should touch the good

it would violate and corrupt it; how impious it is to believe that the nature of evil is powerful enough to change any part of God, and that the Highest Good is corruptible and violable! But if the will was present, assuredly there was present, no one compelling, a movement of the mind either towards not losing something or obtaining something. But this something was either good, or was thought to be good, for not otherwise could it be earnestly desired. But in supreme evil, before the commingling which they maintain, there never was any good. Whence then could there be in it either the knowledge or the thought of good? Did they wish for nothing that was in themselves, and earnestly desire that true good which was without? That will must truly be declared worthy of distinguished and great praise by which is earnestly desired the supreme and true good. Whence then in supreme evil was this movement of mind most worthy of so great praise? Did they seek it for the sake of injuring it? In the first place, the argument comes to the same thing. For he who wishes to injure, wishes to deprive another of some good for the sake of some good of his own. There was therefore in them either a knowledge of good or an opinion of good, which ought by no means to belong to supreme evil. In the second place, whence had they known, that good placed outside of themselves, which they designed to injure, existed at all. If they had intellectually perceived it, what is more excellent than such a mind? Is there anything else for which the whole energy of good men is put forth except the knowledge of that supreme and sincere good? What therefore is now scarcely conceded to a few good and just men, was mere evil, no good assisting, then able to accomplish? But if those souls bore bodies and saw the supreme good with their eyes, what tongues, what hearts, what intellects suffice for lauding and proclaiming those eyes, with which the minds of just men can scarcely be compared? How great good things we find in supreme evil! For if to see God is evil, God is not a good; but God is a good; therefore to see God is good; and I know not what can be compared to this good. Since to see anything is good, whence can it be made out that to be able to see is evil? Therefore whatever in those eyes or in those minds brought it about, that the divine essence could be seen by them, brought about a great thing and a good thing most worthy of ineffable praise. But if it was not brought about, but it was such in itself and eternal, it is difficult to find anything better than this evil.

17. Lastly, that these souls may have nothing of these praiseworthy things which by the reasonings of the Manichæans they are compelled to have, I should have asked, whether God condemns any or no souls. If none, there is no judgment of rewards and punishments, no providence, and the world is administered by chance rather than by reason, or rather is not administered at all. For the name administration must not be given to chances. But if it is impious for all those that are bound by any religion to believe this, it remains either that there is condemnation of some souls, or that there are no sins. But if there are no sins, neither is there any evil. Which if the Manichæans should say, they would slay their heresy with a single blow. Therefore they and I agree that some souls are condemned by divine law and judgment. But if these souls are good, what is that justice? If evil, are they so by nature, or by will? But by nature souls can in no way be evil. Whence do we teach this. From the above definitions of will and sin. For to speak of souls, and that

they are evil, and that they do not sin, is full of madness; but to say that they sin without will, is great craziness, and to hold any one guilty of sin for not doing what he could not do, belongs to the height of iniquity and insanity. Wherefore whatever these souls do, if they do it by nature not by will, that is, if they are wanting in a movement of mind free both for doing and not doing, if finally no power of abstaining from their work is conceded to them; we cannot hold that the sin is theirs. But all confess both that evil souls are justly, and souls that have not sinned are unjustly condemned; therefore they confess that those souls are evil that sin. But these, as reason teaches, do not sin. Therefore the extraneous class of evil souls of the Manichæans, whatever it may be, is a non-entity.

18. Let us now look at that good class of souls, which again they exalt to such a degree as to say that it is the very substance of God. But how much better it is that each one should recognize his own rank and merit, nor be so puffed up with sacrilegious pride as to believe that as often as he experiences a change in himself it is the substance of that supreme good, which devout reason holds and teaches to be unchangeable! For behold! since it is manifest that souls do not sin in not being such as they cannot be; it follows that these supposititious souls, whatever they may be, do not sin at all, and moreover that they are absolutely nonexistent; it remains that since there are sins, they find none to whom to attribute them except the good class of souls and the substance of God. But especially are they pressed by Christian authority; for never have they denied that forgiveness of sins is granted when anyone has been converted to God; never have they said (as they have said of many other passages) that some

corrupter has interpolated this into the divine Scriptures. To whom then are sins attributed? If to those evil souls of the alien class, these also can become good, can possess the kingdom of God with Christ. Which denying, they [the Manichæans] have no other class except those souls which they maintain are of the substance of God. It remains that they acknowledge that not only these latter also, but these alone sin. But I make no contention about their being alone in sinning; yet they sin. But are they compelled to sin by being commingled with evil? If so compelled that there was no power of resisting, they do not sin. If it is in their power to resist, and they voluntarily consent, we are compelled to find out through their [the Manichæan] teaching, why so great good things in supreme evil, why this evil in supreme good, unless it be that neither is that which they bring into suspicion evil, nor is that which they pervert by superstition supreme good?

Chapter 13. —From Deliberation on the Evil and on the Good Part It Results that Two Classes of Souls are Not to Be Held to. A Class of Souls Enticing to Shameful Deeds Having Been Conceded, It Does Not Follow that These are Evil by Nature, that the Others are Supreme Good.

19. But if I had taught, or at any rate had myself learned, that they rave and err regarding those two classes of souls, why should I have thenceforth thought them worthy of being heard or consulted about anything? That I might learn hence, that these two kinds of souls are pointed out, which during deliberation assent puts now on the evil side, now on the good? Why is not this rather the

sign of one soul which by free will can be borne here and there, swayed hither and thither? For it was my own experience to feel that I am one, considering evil and good and choosing one or the other, but for the most part the one pleases, the other is fitting, placed amid which we fluctuate. Nor is it to be wondered at, for we are now so constituted that through the flesh we can be affected by sensual pleasure, and through the spirit by honorable considerations. Am I not therefore compelled to acknowledge two souls? Nay, we can better and with far less difficulty recognize two classes of good things, of which neither is alien from God as its author, one soul acted upon from diverse directions, the lower and the higher, or to speak more correctly, the external and the internal. These are the two classes which a little while ago we considered under the names sensible and intelligible, which we now prefer to call more familiarly carnal and spiritual. But it has been made difficult for us to abstain from carnal things, since our truest bread is spiritual. For with great labor we now eat this bread. For neither without punishment for the sin of transgression have we been changed from immortal into mortal. So it happens, that when we strive after better things, habit formed by connection with the flesh and our sins in some way begin to militate against us and to put obstacles in our way, some foolish persons with most obtuse superstition suspect that there is another kind of souls which is not of God.

20. However even if it be conceded to them that we are enticed to shameful deeds by another inferior kind of souls, they do not thence make it evident that those enticing are evil by nature, or those enticed, supremely good. For it may be, the former of their own will, by

striving after what was not lawful, that is, by sinning, from being good have become evil; and again they may be made good, but in such manner that for a long time they remain in sin, and by a certain occult suasion traduce to themselves other souls. Then, they may not be absolutely evil, but in their own kind, however inferior, they may exercise their own functions without any sin. But those superior souls to whom justice, the directress of things, has assigned a far more excellent activity, if they should wish to follow and to imitate those inferior ones, become evil, not because they imitate evil souls, but because they imitate in an evil way. By the evil souls is done what is proper to them, by the good what is alien to them is striven after. Hence the former remain in their own grade, the latter are plunged into a lower. It is as when men copy after beasts. For the four-footed horse walks beautifully, but if a man on all fours should imitate him, who would think him worthy even of chaff for food? Rightly therefore we generally disapprove of one who imitates, while we approve of him whom he imitates. But we disapprove not because he has not succeeded, but for wishing to succeed at all. For in the horse we approve of that to which by as much as we prefer man, by so much are we offended that he copies after inferior creatures. So among men, however well the crier may do in sending forth his voice, would not the senator be insane, if he should do it even more clearly and better than the crier? Take an illustration from the heavenly bodies: The moon when shining is praised, and by its course and its changes is quite pleasing to those that pay attention to such things. But if the sun should wish to imitate it (for we may feign that it has desires of this sort), who would not be greatly and rightly displeased. From which illustrations I wish it to be understood, that even if there are souls (which meanwhile is left an open question) devoted to bodily offices not by sin but by nature, and even if they are related to us, however inferior they may be, by some inner affinity, they should not be esteemed evil simply because we are evil ourselves in following them and in loving corporeal things. For we sin by loving corporeal things, because by justice we are required and by nature we can love spiritual things, and when we do this we are, in our kind, the best and the happiest.

21. Wherefore what proof does deliberation, violently urged in both directions, now prone to sin, now borne on toward right conduct, furnish, that we are compelled to accept two kinds of souls, the nature of one of which is from God, of the other not; when we are free to conjecture so many other causes of alternating states of mind? But that these things are obscure and are to no purpose pried into by blear-eyed minds, whoever is a good judge of things sees. Wherefore those things rather which have been said regarding the will and sin, those things, I say, that supreme justice permits no man using his reason to be ignorant of, those things which if they were taken from us, there is nothing whence the discipline of virtue may begin, nothing whence it may rise from the death of vices, those things I say considered again and again with sufficient clearness and lucidity convince us that the heresy of the Manichæans is false.

Chapter 14. —Again It is Shown from the Utility of Repenting that Souls are Not by Nature Evil. So Sure a Demonstration is Not Contradicted Except from the Habit of Erring.

22. Like the foregoing considerations is what I shall now say about repenting. For as among all sane people it is agreed, and this the Manichæans themselves not only confess but also teach, that to repent of sin is useful. Why shall I now, in this matter, collect the testimonies of the divine Scriptures, which are scattered throughout their pages? It is also the voice of nature; notice of this thing has escaped no fool. We should be undone, if this were not deeply imbedded in our nature. Someone may say that he does not sin; but no barbarity will dare to say, that if one sins he should not repent of it. This being the case, I ask to which of the two kinds of souls does repenting pertain? I know indeed that it can pertain neither to him who does ill nor to him who cannot do well. Wherefore, that I may use the words of the Manichæans, if a soul of darkness repent of sin, it is not of the substance of supreme evil, if a soul of light, it is not of the substance of supreme good; that disposition of repenting which is profitable testifies alike that the penitent has done ill, and that he could have done well. How, therefore, is there from me nothing of evil, if I have acted unadvisedly, or how can I rightly repent if I have not so done? Hear the other part. How is there from me nothing of good, if in me there is good will, or how do I rightly repent if there is not? Wherefore, either let them deny that there is great utility in repenting, so that they may be driven not only from the Christian name, but from every even imaginary argument for their views, or let

them cease to say and to teach that there are two kinds of souls, one of which has nothing of evil, the other nothing of good; for that whole sect is propped up by this two headed or rather headlong variety of souls.

23. And to me indeed it is sufficient thus to know that the Manichæans err, that I know that sin must be repented of; and yet if now by right of friendship I should accost some one of my friends who still thinks that they are worthy of being listened to, and should say to him: Do you not know that it is useful, when anyone has sinned, to repent? Without hesitation he will swear that he knows. If then I shall have convinced you that Manichæism is false, will you not desire anything more? Let him reply what more he can desire in this matter. Very well, so far. But when I shall have begun to show the sure and necessary arguments which, bound to it with adamantine chains, as the saying is, follow that proposition, and shall have conducted to its conclusion the whole process by which that sect is overthrown, he will deny perhaps that he knows the utility of repenting, which no learned man, no unlearned, is ignorant of, and will rather contend, when we hesitate and deliberate, that two souls in us furnish each its own proper help to the solution of the different parts of the question. O habit of sin! O accompanying penalty of sin! Then you turned me away from the consideration of things so manifest, but you injured me when I did not discern. But now, among my most familiar acquaintances who do not discern, you wound and torment me discerning.

Chapter 15. —He Prays for His Friends Whom He Has Had as Associates in Error.

24. Give heed to these things, I beseech you, dearly beloved. Your dispositions I have well known. If you now concede to me the mind and the reason of any sort of man, these things are far more certain than the things that we seemed to learn or rather were compelled to believe. Great God, God omnipotent, God of supreme goodness, whose right it is to be believed and known to be inviolable and unchangeable. Trinal Unity, whom the Catholic Church worships, as one who have experienced in myself Thy mercy, I supplicate Thee, that Thou wilt not permit those with whom from boyhood I have lived most harmoniously in every relation to dissent from me in Thy worship. I see how it was especially to be expected in this place that I should either even then have defended the Catholic Scriptures attacked by the Manichæans, if as I say, I had been cautious; or I should now show that they can be defended. But in other volumes God will aid my purpose, for the moderate length of this, as I suppose, already asks to be spared.

www.ingramcontent.com/pod-product-compliance
Lightning Source LLC
Chambersburg PA
CBHW052045070526
44584CB00018B/2616